Alberta D. Jones

GAL GUARDIANS SERVANTS OF THE DARK

GAME GUIDE

The Complete Walkthrough, Combat Tactics, and Hidden Secrets to Dominate Every Boss Fight

Chapter 1: Introduction to Gal Guardians: Servants of the Dark

1.1 Overview of the Game

Gal Guardians: Servants of the Dark is a side-scrolling action-platformer developed by Inti Creates, known for their expertise in crafting fast-paced, retro-style games. As a part of the *Gal Guardians* series, this title blends classic Metroidvania exploration with modern gameplay mechanics, making it an engaging experience for both veterans and newcomers to the genre.

Set in a dark and mysterious world filled with demonic creatures, the game follows the story of two demon maid sisters, **Kirika** and **Masha**, who must battle their way through the depths of the Demon Realm to resurrect their fallen master, Demon Lord Maxim. Players will face a variety of challenging enemies, uncover hidden secrets, and unlock powerful abilities while progressing through a beautifully detailed 2D world.

Gameplay Style and Features

Gal Guardians: Servants of the Dark offers a rich combination of **action, exploration, and puzzle-solving**, with a gameplay loop centered around:

- **Character Switching Mechanic** – Players can freely switch between **Kirika** and **Masha**, utilizing their unique abilities to navigate the environment and defeat enemies.

- **Metroidvania Exploration** – The game world consists of interconnected areas, requiring players to backtrack and unlock new paths as they acquire new skills.
- **Fast-Paced Combat** – With **ranged attacks from Kirika** and **melee attacks from Masha**, combat is dynamic and requires strategic decision-making.
- **Upgrade System** – Players can collect materials and unlock upgrades to improve their weapons, skills, and abilities.
- **Multiplayer Co-op** – The game supports **local and online co-op**, allowing two players to team up, each controlling one of the sisters.

Visual and Audio Presentation

The game features a **gothic anime-inspired art style**, with **hand-drawn 2D sprite animations** and **detailed environments** that create an immersive dark fantasy atmosphere. The character designs reflect the personalities of Kirika and Masha, while the enemy designs range from grotesque demons to massive, intimidating bosses.

The soundtrack is composed of **orchestral and rock-inspired tracks**, enhancing the tension and excitement during battles while setting an eerie tone in exploration sequences. Voice acting and sound effects further bring the world to life, with each attack, spell, and enemy growl adding to the immersive experience.

Target Audience and Appeal

The game is designed for fans of **Metroidvania games, classic action-platformers, and anime-inspired storytelling.** Whether you're looking for **challenging combat, deep exploration, or co-op gameplay**, *Gal Guardians: Servants of the Dark* provides an engaging experience that caters to different playstyles.

1.2 Story and Setting

The Premise

Gal Guardians: Servants of the Dark follows the journey of two demon maid sisters, **Kirika** and **Masha**, who serve their fallen master, **Demon Lord Maxim**. After a devastating battle, Maxim is slain, and his soul is shattered into fragments, scattered across the **Demon Realm**.

Determined to resurrect their master, Kirika and Masha set out on a perilous mission to retrieve his essence. However, they are not the only ones seeking Maxim's power—rival demons, ancient warriors, and the legendary **Hunters' Order** stand in their way. As they journey deeper into the Demon Realm, they uncover dark secrets about their master's past and the true forces at play behind his downfall.

The Demon Realm: A World of Darkness

The game is set in the **Demon Realm**, a vast, interconnected world filled with cursed castles, haunted ruins, and supernatural dangers. Each area presents unique challenges, enemies, and hidden paths that reward exploration.

Key Locations:

- **The Abyssal Fortress** – The central hub and former seat of Demon Lord Maxim's power, now overrun by rival demon factions.
- **The Crimson Catacombs** – A labyrinthine underground dungeon filled with restless spirits, deadly traps, and lost relics.

- **The Ruins of the Forgotten Ones** – A shattered kingdom that fell to demonic corruption, containing lost knowledge and hidden passageways.
- **The Eclipse Tower** – A towering spire guarded by Maxim's former generals, offering brutal battles and shocking revelations.

Each location is designed with **Metroidvania-style exploration**, requiring players to unlock new abilities to access hidden areas and uncover Maxim's scattered soul fragments.

Allies and Rivals

As Kirika and Masha progress, they encounter a cast of **allies, enemies, and mysterious figures** with their own agendas:

- **Demon Lord Maxim** – The sisters' fallen master, whose fate is at the heart of their mission.
- **Lady Selene** – A powerful witch who once served Maxim but now seeks to claim his power for herself.
- **The Hunters' Order** – An elite group of demon hunters determined to eradicate all demonkind.
- **Rival Demon Generals** – Maxim's former warriors who have turned against him and now fight for control of the Demon Realm.

The Mystery Behind Maxim's Death

As the sisters collect Maxim's soul fragments, they begin to unravel a disturbing truth—was Maxim truly betrayed, or was a greater force responsible for his downfall?

1.3 Main Characters: Kirika & Masha

Kirika – The Deadeye Maid

Kirika is the elder of the two demon maid sisters and the more composed and tactical fighter. She specializes in **long-range combat**, utilizing enchanted firearms that allow her to keep enemies at a distance while dealing precise damage.

Personality and Background

- Kirika is **calm, intelligent, and highly disciplined**, serving as the more strategic and level-headed sister.
- She has a **deep sense of loyalty** to Demon Lord Maxim and will stop at nothing to resurrect him.
- While she appears emotionless, she deeply cares for Masha and often plays the role of a protective older sister.
- Kirika values efficiency and prefers to analyze situations before engaging in battle.

Combat Abilities

- **Demonic Firearms** – Uses twin magical guns to fire projectiles at enemies.
- **Precision Sniping** – Can charge shots for increased damage.
- **Elemental Bullets** – Unlocks different ammo types (fire, ice, lightning) to exploit enemy weaknesses.
- **Shadow Evasion** – A quick dash move that allows her to dodge attacks and reposition strategically.

Strengths & Weaknesses

- Best at long-range combat, allowing her to attack from a safe distance.

- Excellent mobility and evasion tactics.
- Versatile with different bullet types for different enemy weaknesses.
- Lower health compared to Masha, making her more vulnerable in close-range fights.
- Weaker melee attacks, relying on spacing and positioning.

Masha – The Crimson Executioner

Masha is the younger and more aggressive of the two sisters. Unlike Kirika, she excels in **close-quarters combat**, wielding a deadly **demonic whip** to tear through enemies with fast, sweeping strikes.

Personality and Background

- Masha is **hot-headed, impulsive, and battle-hungry**, always looking for a fight.
- She is **fiercely protective** of Kirika, often putting herself in harm's way to defend her sister.
- Despite her brash nature, she is highly skilled and possesses a deep respect for strength and honor.
- Masha sees their mission as a **personal vendetta**, eager to punish those responsible for Maxim's downfall.

Combat Abilities

- **Demonic Whip Mastery** – Uses a long, enchanted whip to deal **AoE (area-of-effect) damage** to multiple enemies.
- **Blood Surge** – Can unleash a **frenzied attack mode**, increasing her attack speed for a short duration.
- **Grapple Hook** – Uses her whip to swing across gaps and access high ledges.
- **Rage Counter** – A parry move that allows her to block an enemy attack and counter with a devastating strike.

Strengths & Weaknesses

- High damage output with rapid melee attacks.
- Can hit multiple enemies at once with wide-range whip strikes.
- Whip doubles as a traversal tool, helping her navigate platforming sections.
- Vulnerable to long-range enemies due to limited projectile options.
- Requires aggressive playstyle, making her more exposed to damage.

Character Synergy & Switching Mechanics

Kirika and Masha complement each other's combat styles, allowing players to switch between them on the fly:

- Use **Kirika** to deal with long-range threats, weaken enemies, and avoid unnecessary risks.
- Switch to **Masha** for close-range brawls, taking down groups of enemies and breaking through defenses.

1.4 Game Mechanics and Playstyle

Core Gameplay Mechanics

Gal Guardians: Servants of the Dark blends **Metroidvania-style exploration, fast-paced action combat, and puzzle-solving** with a unique **character-switching system**. Players control **Kirika** and **Masha**, utilizing their distinct abilities to progress through the Demon Realm, defeat powerful enemies, and uncover hidden secrets.

Character Switching System

- Players can **freely switch** between Kirika and Masha at any time, each offering different combat styles and abilities.
- **Kirika excels in ranged combat**, using magical firearms to deal precise damage from a distance.
- **Masha specializes in melee attacks**, wielding a deadly whip for close-range battles and traversal.
- Certain puzzles and enemy encounters **require switching characters** to exploit weaknesses or navigate obstacles.

Combat System

The game features a **fast and responsive combat system**, requiring players to adapt their strategies based on enemy types and environmental hazards.

Attack Styles

- **Kirika**: Uses **twin pistols** with elemental bullets for long-range attacks. Can charge shots for **sniper-like precision**.
- **Masha**: Wields a **demonic whip** for **fast melee combos and area-of-effect (AoE) attacks**. Also has a parry mechanic for countering enemies.

Special Abilities

- **Dodge & Counter** – Both characters can evade attacks, but Masha can **parry** melee strikes for a powerful counterattack.
- **Magic Skills** – Unlockable abilities allow both characters to use **dark magic**, enhancing attacks or summoning temporary buffs.
- **Ultimate Attacks** – A powerful, character-specific move that requires a fully charged energy bar to unleash.

Enemy Encounters & Boss Fights

- Regular enemies vary from **lesser demons to elite warriors**, each with different attack patterns and weaknesses.
- **Mini-bosses guard key locations**, testing players' skills before progressing further.
- **Major boss battles** feature multi-phase encounters that require pattern recognition and adaptive strategies.

Exploration and Level Design

The world is **semi-open**, featuring interconnected regions with **hidden paths, locked doors, and environmental hazards**.

Metroidvania Elements

- Progression is **non-linear**, requiring players to revisit areas with newly acquired abilities.
- **Hidden shortcuts and secret rooms** provide powerful upgrades and collectibles.
- Some areas require **character-specific skills**, such as Kirika's ranged precision or Masha's whip-based traversal.

Puzzle-Solving & Environmental Interactions

- Puzzles may require **activating switches, platforming challenges, or manipulating objects**.
- Certain enemies drop **keys or magical relics** needed to access blocked paths.
- **Light and shadow mechanics** influence enemy behavior and can be used strategically.

Upgrade and Progression System

The game features an **RPG-lite progression system**, allowing players to enhance their characters' abilities.

Skill Trees

- **Kirika's Skill Tree** – Focuses on **firearm upgrades, elemental bullet enhancements, and evasive maneuvers**.
- **Masha's Skill Tree** – Enhances **whip damage, parrying strength, and melee combos**.

Item Collection & Crafting

- Players can **collect rare materials** to craft **weapon upgrades, health potions, and magic enhancers**.
- Defeating mini-bosses grants **unique relics** that provide passive buffs.

Multiplayer and Co-op Mode

- The game features a **local and online co-op mode**, where players control **Kirika and Masha simultaneously**.
- Co-op introduces **team-based puzzles and synchronized attacks**, encouraging collaboration.
- Certain enemy encounters scale in difficulty based on **single-player or co-op mode**.

Final Thoughts on Playstyle

Players can **choose their preferred playstyle**, whether focusing on:

- **Kirika's precise, long-range combat** and tactical positioning.
- **Masha's aggressive, melee-focused approach** with fast, high-damage combos.
- A **balanced playstyle**, switching characters based on combat situations and puzzle-solving needs.

Chapter 2: Getting Started

2.1 System Requirements and Platforms

Available Platforms

Gal Guardians: Servants of the Dark is available on multiple gaming platforms, ensuring a broad range of accessibility for players. The game supports:

- **PC (Windows & Steam Deck)**
- **PlayStation 4 & PlayStation 5**
- **Xbox One & Xbox Series X/S**
- **Nintendo Switch**

Each platform offers optimized performance, with some featuring enhanced graphics, faster load times, and additional controller support.

Minimum and Recommended System Requirements (PC)

For PC players, ensuring that their system meets the required specifications is essential for smooth gameplay. Below are the **minimum** and **recommended** system requirements:

Minimum Requirements

- **OS:** Windows 10 (64-bit)
- **Processor:** Intel Core i5-7500 / AMD Ryzen 3 1200
- **Memory:** 8 GB RAM
- **Graphics:** NVIDIA GTX 960 / AMD Radeon R7 370

- **Storage:** 15 GB available space
- **DirectX:** Version 11
- **Additional Notes:** A stable internet connection is required for online co-op features.

Recommended Requirements

- **OS:** Windows 11 (64-bit)
- **Processor:** Intel Core i7-9700 / AMD Ryzen 5 3600
- **Memory:** 16 GB RAM
- **Graphics:** NVIDIA GTX 1660 Ti / AMD Radeon RX 5600 XT
- **Storage:** 15 GB SSD for faster load times
- **DirectX:** Version 12
- **Additional Notes:** A gamepad is recommended for the best experience.

Performance on Consoles

The game runs smoothly on **current-gen and last-gen consoles**, with some key differences:

- **PlayStation 5 & Xbox Series X/S**:
  - Supports **4K resolution and 60 FPS**.
  - Faster loading times with SSD support.
  - Improved lighting and particle effects.
- **PlayStation 4 & Xbox One**:
  - Runs at **1080p with 30-60 FPS**, depending on the scene.
  - Slightly longer loading times.
- **Nintendo Switch**:
  - Runs at **900p docked / 720p handheld** at **30 FPS**.
  - Minor graphical downgrades to maintain stable performance.

Gamepad and Control Support

- Full support for **keyboard and mouse** on PC, but a **controller is highly recommended** for optimal gameplay.
- Supports **DualSense (PS5), Xbox controllers, and Nintendo Pro Controller** with haptic feedback and adaptive triggers enabled on supported hardware.
- Fully customizable button mapping to suit player preferences.

2.2 Game Modes and Difficulty Settings

Game Modes

Gal Guardians: Servants of the Dark offers multiple gameplay modes, catering to different playstyles and levels of challenge. Whether playing solo or with a friend, the game provides a variety of ways to experience its dark and action-packed adventure.

1. Story Mode (Single-Player Campaign)

- The **main mode** of the game, where players follow the journey of **Kirika and Masha** through the **Demon Realm**.
- Features **Metroidvania-style exploration, puzzles, and intense boss battles**.
- Players can freely **switch between Kirika and Masha**, using their unique abilities to overcome obstacles.
- **Save points and checkpoints** allow players to track progress and recover health.

2. Co-op Mode (Local & Online Multiplayer)

- Allows two players to **control Kirika and Masha simultaneously**, promoting teamwork.
- Features **co-op-exclusive mechanics**, such as synchronized attacks and puzzle-solving elements.
- **Drop-in/drop-out multiplayer**, meaning a second player can join or leave at any time.
- Online multiplayer supports **voice chat and quick commands** for better coordination.

3. Boss Rush Mode

- Unlocks after completing the main campaign.
- Players face **back-to-back battles** against all major bosses.
- Time is recorded for **leaderboard rankings** (online mode only).
- Can be played with either **Kirika, Masha, or both** in co-op mode.

4. Hardcore Mode (Permadeath Challenge)

- **Unlocked after the first playthrough.**
- **No checkpoints, no extra lives, and limited healing options.**
- Enemies and bosses are **more aggressive and deal increased damage**.
- Only for experienced players seeking the ultimate challenge.

Difficulty Settings

Players can adjust the difficulty before starting the game, catering to casual players and hardcore veterans alike.

1. Casual Mode *(For Beginners & Story-Focused Players)*

- Enemies deal **reduced damage**, and player health is increased.
- **Unlimited continues** with **more frequent checkpoints**.
- **Auto-healing over time** (outside of combat).
- **Hints and guidance** provided for puzzles.

2. Normal Mode *(Balanced Experience – Default Setting)*

- Standard difficulty with **fair enemy AI and damage scaling**.
- Checkpoints are present, but **healing items are limited**.
- Requires **strategic use of character-switching** to survive battles.
- Enemies have **predictable attack patterns but require skill to defeat**.

3. Veteran Mode *(For Experienced Action Players)*

- Enemies are **faster, stronger, and more aggressive**.
- **Healing items are rare**, and checkpoints are **less frequent**.
- Bosses have **additional attack phases** and **unpredictable moves**.
- **Perfect dodging and counterattacks** are crucial for survival.

4. Nightmare Mode *(Extreme Challenge – Unlockable after Beating Veteran Mode)*

- Enemies **one-shot the player** in most situations.

- **No checkpoints** – only manual saves at safe zones.
- **Limited inventory space**, forcing careful resource management.
- Bosses have **entirely new attack patterns** and are **twice as fast**.
- Designed for **hardcore players looking for the ultimate test**.

2.3 Understanding the HUD and Controls

Mastering the **Heads-Up Display (HUD) and controls** is essential for navigating the world of *Gal Guardians: Servants of the Dark*. The HUD provides crucial information, while the controls allow players to execute precise actions during combat and exploration.

Heads-Up Display (HUD) Overview

The HUD in *Gal Guardians: Servants of the Dark* is designed to provide key gameplay information in a non-intrusive way. Below are the main elements of the HUD and their functions:

1. Health Bar (Top Left Corner)

- Displays the **current HP** of the active character.
- A **green bar** represents remaining health, while a **flashing red bar** indicates critical health status.
- Health values are separate for Kirika and Masha, so switching characters strategically can help manage damage.

2. Energy Bar (Below Health Bar)

- Represents the resource used for **special attacks and abilities**.

- Energy regenerates slowly over time or can be replenished by collecting energy orbs.
- Some powerful moves consume larger amounts of energy, requiring careful management.

3. Character Portraits & Switch Indicator

- Shows **Kirika and Masha's portraits**, helping players track who is currently active.
- A **cooldown timer** appears after switching characters, preventing excessive swaps.

4. Weapon & Ammo Display (Bottom Right Corner)

- When playing as **Kirika**, this section shows the **current ammo type and remaining bullets**.
- When controlling **Masha**, it displays the **whip charge level** for enhanced melee attacks.

5. Mini-Map (Top Right Corner)

- Provides an **overview of explored areas and nearby objectives**.
- Locked doors, treasure chests, and critical points of interest are marked.
- Players can **zoom in** to examine details and plan their next move.

6. Enemy Health Bar (Above Enemies & Bosses)

- Standard enemies display **a small health bar above their heads**.
- Bosses have **larger, segmented health bars** at the top of the screen, making it easier to track their remaining health during battles.

7. Status Effects & Buffs (Bottom Left Corner)

- Displays any **active status effects**, such as poison, slow, or burn.
- Shows **temporary power-ups**, including attack boosts or defensive shields.

Controls Guide (Default Layouts)

Understanding the controls is key to mastering combat and exploration. Below is the standard control scheme for each platform:

Console Controls (PlayStation, Xbox, Switch)

- Move using the **left analog stick.**
- Jump by pressing **X (PlayStation), A (Xbox), or B (Switch).**
- Attack with **Square (PlayStation), X (Xbox), or Y (Switch).**
- Perform a special attack using **Triangle (PlayStation), Y (Xbox), or X (Switch).**
- Dodge or parry with **Circle (PlayStation), B (Xbox), or A (Switch).**
- Switch characters using **L1 (PlayStation), LB (Xbox), or L (Switch).**
- Use items by pressing **R1 (PlayStation), RB (Xbox), or R (Switch).**
- Open the map menu with **the touchpad (PlayStation), the view button (Xbox), or the minus (-) button (Switch).**

PC Keyboard & Mouse Controls (Default Settings)

- Move with **W, A, S, D.**
- Jump using **Spacebar.**
- Attack with **Left Click.**
- Perform a special attack with **Right Click.**

- Dodge or parry by pressing **Shift**.
- Switch characters with **Tab**.
- Use items with **E**.
- Open the map menu using **M**.

Additional Notes on Controls:

- The game allows **full control customization** in the settings menu, so players can adjust inputs to their preference.
- **Gamepads are highly recommended** for better movement precision and smoother combat, especially for platforming sections.

2.4 Starting Your First Playthrough

Starting your journey in *Gal Guardians: Servants of the Dark* can be both exciting and challenging. This section will guide you through the essential steps to begin your adventure, including selecting the right difficulty, understanding key mechanics, and making the most of your first experience.

1. Selecting Game Mode and Difficulty

Before jumping into the game, you'll need to choose your **game mode** and **difficulty setting**.

- **Story Mode (Single-Player Campaign):** The main adventure where you control Kirika and Masha through the demon-infested castle.
- **Co-op Mode (Local & Online Multiplayer):** Play alongside a friend, with each player controlling one sister.
- **Boss Rush Mode:** Available after completing the main game, this mode challenges players to defeat all bosses in succession.

- **Hardcore Mode (Permadeath):** A brutal challenge mode unlocked after beating the game once.

For first-time players, it is recommended to start with **Normal Mode** for a balanced experience. If you prefer an easier time focusing on the story, **Casual Mode** is a good option. If you're a veteran action-platformer player, **Veteran Mode** will provide a greater challenge.

2. Character Selection and Playstyle

In *Gal Guardians: Servants of the Dark*, you control both **Kirika** and **Masha**, each with unique abilities and combat styles.

- **Kirika:** A ranged fighter who specializes in firearms. She excels at attacking from a distance and is best for handling enemies before they get too close.
- **Masha:** A melee warrior who wields a powerful whip. She is better suited for close-quarters combat and can deal high damage up close.

Switching between characters strategically is crucial, especially when encountering enemies with different attack patterns. Learning how and when to swap between the two will improve your survival chances.

3. Exploring the First Area

Once you start the game, you'll be introduced to the **first level**, which serves as a tutorial area. Here's what you should focus on:

- **Learn the Basic Movements:** Moving, jumping, dodging, and attacking are fundamental to survival.

- **Understand Enemy Patterns:** Early enemies have predictable attack patterns. Use this time to practice dodging and counterattacking.
- **Break Objects for Loot:** Destroy crates, barrels, and lanterns to collect **health pickups, ammo, and energy orbs**.
- **Interact with the Environment:** Certain platforms, levers, and doors may require character-specific interactions.

Take your time exploring the tutorial area, as it introduces mechanics that will be essential later in the game.

4. Managing Resources and Items

Throughout your adventure, you'll collect various resources that can help you survive.

- **Health Items:** These restore HP and should be saved for critical moments.
- **Energy Orbs:** Used for special attacks and abilities. Always keep an eye on your energy bar.
- **Ammunition:** Kirika's firearms require ammo, which is found by defeating enemies or breaking objects.
- **Keys & Quest Items:** Some doors and pathways are locked until you find the necessary items.

Understanding how to manage your **health, energy, and inventory** will be essential as you progress.

5. First Mini-Boss Encounter

Shortly after the tutorial, you will face your **first mini-boss**. This encounter is designed to test your ability to switch between Kirika and Masha effectively.

Tips for Success:

- **Observe the boss's attack patterns** before committing to aggressive moves.
- **Dodge and counterattack** when an opening presents itself.
- **Use character switching** to avoid damage and maximize attack efficiency.
- **Keep an eye on your health and energy**—use items if necessary.

Defeating the first mini-boss successfully will prepare you for more intense battles ahead.

6. Saving and Checkpoints

Progress in *Gal Guardians: Servants of the Dark* is maintained through **checkpoints and save points** scattered throughout the game.

- **Checkpoints:** If you lose a life, you will respawn at the last checkpoint.
- **Save Rooms:** These allow you to fully restore health and save progress. They are usually found before difficult encounters.

Chapter 3: Combat Mechanics

3.1 Kirika's Ranged Attacks and Strategies

Kirika specializes in **ranged combat**, utilizing firearms to attack enemies from a distance. Her **long-range attacks** allow her to deal damage while avoiding direct confrontation, making her ideal for handling airborne or fast-moving enemies.

Basic Attacks

- **Standard Shot:** Fires a quick burst of bullets with moderate damage and range.
- **Charged Shot:** Holding the attack button allows Kirika to charge her weapon for a more powerful, piercing shot.
- **Spread Shot (Upgrade):** Fires multiple bullets in a wider arc, effective for clearing groups of enemies.

Combat Strategies

- **Keep Your Distance:** Kirika is most effective when fighting from afar. Use high ground or ledges to maintain an advantage over melee enemies.
- **Manage Ammo Efficiently:** Some weapons require ammo, which is limited. Be mindful of your shots and look for pickups.
- **Aim for Weak Points:** Certain enemies have weak spots that take extra damage. Target these for faster kills.
- **Utilize Cover:** Use the environment to avoid incoming attacks while continuing to fire at enemies.

3.2 Masha's Melee Combat Techniques

Masha is a **close-range fighter**, using her whip to strike enemies with powerful melee attacks. She is best for **high-damage output** and dealing with enemies that resist ranged attacks.

Basic Attacks

- **Standard Whip Strike:** A fast melee attack with good range.
- **Combo Attack:** Pressing the attack button repeatedly unleashes a multi-hit combo.
- **Heavy Strike:** A slower, charged attack that deals more damage and can break enemy defenses.

Combat Strategies

- **Stay Aggressive:** Masha's whip attacks deal more damage than Kirika's bullets but require getting close. Stay on the offensive to prevent enemies from counterattacking.
- **Use Dodge Effectively:** Masha has a **faster dodge roll** than Kirika, allowing her to evade enemy attacks quickly.
- **Break Shields:** Some enemies have shields that deflect bullets. Masha's heavy attack can break these defenses.
- **Air Combos:** Masha can juggle enemies in the air, keeping them from retaliating while dealing extra damage.

3.3 Switching Between Characters Effectively

Switching between **Kirika and Masha** at the right moment is key to mastering combat. Each sister excels in different scenarios, and knowing when to swap can be the difference between victory and defeat.

When to Switch

- **Against Flying or Distant Enemies:** Use Kirika's ranged attacks to deal with airborne threats safely.
- **Against Armored or Shielded Enemies:** Masha's melee attacks can break through defenses that Kirika's bullets cannot.
- **When Low on Health:** If one character is low on HP, switch to the other to avoid unnecessary risk.
- **For Puzzle Solving:** Some environmental challenges require one character's specific ability to progress.

Advanced Switching Tactics

- **Combo Swapping:** Attack with Kirika from a distance, then immediately switch to Masha for a finishing melee strike.
- **Escape Swaps:** If an enemy gets too close to Kirika, switch to Masha and dodge away.
- **Energy Conservation:** Use Kirika's special attacks while Masha's energy regenerates, then swap to Masha to use her abilities.

Mastering the **character-switching mechanic** makes combat more fluid and allows for creative strategies.

3.4 Special Attacks and Abilities

Both Kirika and Masha have **special attacks** that consume **energy** but deal massive damage. These moves are crucial in tough battles, especially against bosses.

Kirika's Special Abilities

- **Sniper Shot:** Fires a high-powered shot that pierces through multiple enemies.
- **Explosive Rounds:** Shoots a grenade-like projectile that explodes on impact.
- **Freeze Bullets:** Temporarily slows down enemies, making them easier to hit.

Masha's Special Abilities

- **Whip Slam:** A devastating ground slam that damages all nearby enemies.
- **Chain Grab:** Pulls enemies toward her for close-range combos.
- **Berserker Mode:** Temporarily increases attack speed and damage.

Using Special Attacks Effectively

- **Save Energy for Bosses:** Special attacks deal heavy damage, so use them strategically during difficult fights.
- **Combine Abilities:** Freezing an enemy with Kirika before switching to Masha for a powerful melee combo can be a great tactic.
- **Watch Energy Levels:** Energy does not regenerate quickly, so avoid wasting special attacks on weak enemies.

Chapter 4: Exploring the Demon Realm

4.1 Map Navigation and Hidden Areas

Exploring the **Demon Realm** in *Gal Guardians: Servants of the Dark* requires mastering map navigation and uncovering hidden areas filled with secrets, shortcuts, and valuable rewards.

Understanding the Map System

The **mini-map** in the top-right corner of the screen provides a **real-time layout** of the area, while the **main map** (accessible from the pause menu) gives a **detailed view of all discovered locations**.

- **Blue Rooms:** Explored areas where no threats remain.
- **Red Rooms:** Unexplored or enemy-filled locations.
- **Green Icons:** Save rooms where players can restore health and save progress.
- **Yellow Icons:** Key points of interest, such as objectives, boss rooms, or NPCs.

The map updates as you progress, marking **locked doors, shortcuts, and secret pathways**. Always check it after acquiring new abilities, as they may allow access to previously unreachable areas.

Discovering Hidden Areas

The Demon Realm is filled with **hidden paths, breakable walls, and secret rooms** containing treasures, upgrades, and lore entries.

- **Breakable Walls:** Some walls can be destroyed using **Masha's heavy attack** or **Kirika's explosive rounds**.
- **Illusionary Walls:** Certain sections may appear solid but disappear upon interaction or attack.
- **Secret Passages:** Pay attention to **cracks in the walls** or **slightly misaligned bricks**, as they often indicate hidden entrances.
- **Platforming Challenges:** Some areas require precise jumping or the use of **character abilities** to access.

4.2 Environmental Hazards and How to Overcome Them

The Demon Realm is a treacherous place filled with **deadly environmental hazards** designed to test your reflexes and problem-solving skills. Learning how to navigate these obstacles is essential for survival.

Common Hazards and How to Avoid Them

1. Spike Traps

- Spikes deal heavy damage upon contact and can instantly end a run in some difficulty modes.
- **Solution:** Time your jumps carefully or use **Masha's air dash ability** to clear large gaps.

2. Lava & Poison Pools

- Some areas are covered in burning lava or toxic poison that continuously drains health.

- **Solution:** Look for **floating platforms** or use **Kirika's long-range attacks** to clear threats from a safe distance before advancing.

3. Collapsing Platforms

- Certain platforms crumble after standing on them for too long.
- **Solution:** Move quickly and chain jumps to avoid falling into danger.

4. Falling Objects

- Chandeliers, boulders, or debris may suddenly drop when you step underneath them.
- **Solution:** Watch for shadows or cracks in the ceiling as a warning sign.

5. Darkness Zones

- Some areas are completely dark, limiting visibility and hiding enemies.
- **Solution:** Look for **light sources** or use **special abilities** that illuminate surroundings.

Using Character Abilities to Overcome Hazards

- **Masha's Whip Grab:** Can latch onto hooks to swing across dangerous gaps.
- **Kirika's Freeze Bullets:** Can **solidify lava** temporarily, creating new platforms.
- **Double Jump & Air Dash:** Essential for clearing large chasms or dodging falling traps.

4.3 Backtracking and Unlocking New Paths

As you progress through *Gal Guardians: Servants of the Dark*, you'll encounter areas that are **inaccessible at first** due to locked doors, impassable obstacles, or platforming challenges. **Backtracking** is a key gameplay element, allowing you to return to previous locations with **new abilities** to unlock hidden secrets and shortcuts.

Why Backtracking is Important

- **Unlocking New Areas:** Some doors and pathways require **specific abilities or items** to access.
- **Finding Hidden Treasures:** Upgrades, health expansions, and special weapons are often found in previously inaccessible areas.
- **Shortcut Creation:** Discovering **alternate routes** can make revisiting certain regions easier.
- **Completing Side Quests:** Some NPCs or objectives require you to return to earlier areas after gaining new powers.

Key Abilities That Unlock Paths

As you advance, you'll acquire special abilities that grant access to previously blocked areas:

- **Double Jump:** Helps reach high ledges and hidden platforms.
- **Wall Climb:** Allows vertical traversal on certain surfaces.
- **Whip Grab (Masha):** Can latch onto hooks and pull herself across large gaps.
- **Explosive Rounds (Kirika):** Destroys certain barriers and weak walls.

- **Water Walk:** Enables movement across hazardous liquids like lava or poison.

Tips for Effective Backtracking

- **Mark Unreachable Areas:** Take note of places where you couldn't progress before.
- **Check the Map Frequently:** Newly acquired abilities can open doors or paths you may have forgotten about.
- **Look for Visual Cues:** Cracked walls, suspicious gaps, or unmarked doors often hint at hidden areas.
- **Explore Thoroughly:** Some backtracking rewards are optional but provide **powerful upgrades**.

4.4 Fast Travel and Checkpoints

Navigating the vast Demon Realm can be time-consuming, but the game provides **fast travel and checkpoint systems** to make movement easier.

Fast Travel System

Fast travel allows players to **quickly move between key locations** without having to manually traverse every area again.

- **Fast Travel Points:** These are scattered throughout the game and often located in **safe rooms** or near major objectives.
- **Activation Required:** Some fast travel stations must be **unlocked manually** before they can be used.
- **Limited Destinations:** Early in the game, only a few locations are accessible, but more unlock as you progress.

Using fast travel wisely helps with **efficient backtracking,** especially when hunting for collectibles or completing side objectives.

Checkpoint System

Checkpoints serve as **respawn locations** in case of death, ensuring you don't lose too much progress.

- **Save Rooms:** Found in **safe zones**, allowing full HP restoration and manual saving.
- **Mid-Level Checkpoints:** Some areas have **auto-save markers**, preventing players from restarting an entire level after failure.
- **Pre-Boss Checkpoints:** Before major battles, the game provides a **nearby save or checkpoint**, allowing retries without excessive backtracking.

How to Use Checkpoints and Fast Travel Effectively

- **Save Before Boss Fights:** Always use a **save room** before entering a boss arena.
- **Plan Your Routes:** Fast travel makes collecting missed items much faster—use it wisely.
- **Restock on Items:** Before teleporting to a dangerous area, ensure you have enough **health and ammo.**
- **Memorize Safe Zones:** Knowing where **healing points and checkpoints** are located can be crucial in tough sections.

Chapter 5: Enemies and Boss Battles

5.1 Common Enemies and Their Weaknesses

Throughout *Gal Guardians: Servants of the Dark*, players will face a variety of **demonic creatures**, each with different attack patterns, strengths, and weaknesses. Learning how to counter them effectively is key to survival.

Basic Enemy Types

1. **Lesser Demons (Grunts)**
   - **Attack Style:** Slow-moving melee attacks.
   - **Weakness:** Easily staggered by **Masha's melee combos**.
   - **Strategy:** Use quick whip attacks or keep your distance with Kirika's ranged shots.
2. **Gargoyle Sentinels**
   - **Attack Style:** Flies overhead and swoops down to attack.
   - **Weakness:** Vulnerable to **Kirika's long-range attacks**.
   - **Strategy: Aim upwards and fire** before they get too close.
3. **Cursed Swordsmen**
   - **Attack Style:** Uses **swift sword slashes** and blocks bullets.
   - **Weakness:** Can't block **Masha's heavy attacks**.

- Strategy: Break their guard with a **whip slam**, then follow up with rapid strikes.
4. **Exploding Wraiths**
   - **Attack Style:** Floats toward players before self-destructing.
   - **Weakness:** Destroyed from a distance.
   - **Strategy: Always attack from afar** using Kirika's bullets.
5. **Poison Spiders**
   - **Attack Style:** Drops venom that creates toxic puddles.
   - **Weakness:** Weak to **fire-based attacks**.
   - **Strategy:** Avoid stepping in poison and eliminate them **before they land**.
6. **Shadow Stalkers**
   - **Attack Style:** Teleports behind the player for surprise attacks.
   - **Weakness:** Vulnerable **right before teleporting**.
   - **Strategy:** Dodge roll just before they strike, then counterattack.

5.2 Mini-Bosses and Sub-Boss Encounters

Mini-bosses and sub-bosses serve as **mid-level challenges** that test the player's ability to react, switch characters strategically, and use special abilities effectively.

Notable Mini-Bosses

1. **The Possessed Knight**
   - **Attacks:** Powerful sword slashes and shield blocks.

- Weakness: Slow movement makes it vulnerable to **Kirika's hit-and-run tactics**.
- Strategy: Bait its **heavy attacks**, dodge, then counterattack.

2. **The Twin Gargoyle Guardians**
   - **Attacks:** One shoots fireballs while the other charges with melee attacks.
   - **Weakness:** Attacks leave them vulnerable to **coordinated strikes**.
   - **Strategy:** Defeat the **ranged one first** while dodging the melee attacker.

3. **The Venomous Widow**
   - **Attacks:** Spawns spider minions and spits acid.
   - **Weakness: Fire-based attacks** deal extra damage.
   - **Strategy:** Keep moving, eliminate minions first, and attack when she stops to summon more.

4. **The Shadow Reaver**
   - **Attacks:** Warps around the battlefield, creating illusion clones.
   - **Weakness:** Clones disappear when **hit once**.
   - **Strategy:** Use **Masha's area attacks** to clear illusions quickly before focusing on the real boss.

Tips for Defeating Mini-Bosses

- **Observe Patterns:** Most mini-bosses have **predictable attack cycles**—learning them will give you an advantage.
- **Switch Characters Strategically:** If one character is struggling, switch to the other for a different approach.
- **Use Special Abilities Wisely: Save energy attacks** for moments when the boss is most vulnerable.
- **Watch for Health Drops:** Some mini-bosses spawn **small healing orbs** after certain phases—grab them when needed.

5.3 Major Boss Battles and Strategies

Major boss battles in *Gal Guardians: Servants of the Dark* are **challenging encounters** that require precise timing, character switching, and mastery of special abilities. Each boss has **unique attack patterns, weaknesses, and multiple phases**, making each fight a true test of skill.

Key Boss Battle Strategies

1. **Study Attack Patterns**
   - Bosses have **predictable attack sequences**—observe their movements and attack only during openings.
   - Learn **phase transitions**—as bosses lose health, they often **gain new attacks**.
2. **Use Character Switching Efficiently**
   - **Kirika:** Best for **long-range damage** and evading melee-based bosses.
   - **Masha:** Strong against **slow bosses with armor-breaking attacks**.
   - Swap **right before a heavy attack lands** to avoid unnecessary damage.
3. **Utilize the Environment**
   - Some arenas have **platforms or cover** that can be used to avoid attacks.
   - Watch for **healing or energy pickups** that may appear mid-fight.
4. **Save Special Abilities for Critical Moments**
   - Some bosses enter **"weakened states"** where they take extra damage—this is the best time to unleash **Kirika's sniper shot** or **Masha's whip slam**.
5. **Dodge and Counterattack**

- Most bosses have **telegraphed attacks**—dodge at the right moment, then punish them with a combo.
- **Rolling and jumping** at the right time can avoid massive damage.

Notable Major Bosses & How to Beat Them

1. The Bloodstained Countess (Vampire Queen)

- **Attacks:** Summons bats, teleports, and performs a devastating life-drain attack.
- **Weakness:** Light-based attacks and ranged firepower.
- **Strategy:**
  - Use **Kirika's explosive rounds** to take out bats quickly.
  - Keep moving to **avoid life-drain attacks**.
  - Attack when she reappears after teleporting.

2. The Abyssal Behemoth (Giant Shadow Beast)

- **Attacks:** Charges across the stage, summons shadow tentacles, and creates shockwaves.
- **Weakness:** Vulnerable after a charge attack.
- **Strategy:**
  - **Dodge its charge** and strike from behind.
  - Use **Masha's heavy attack** to break tentacles before they overwhelm the field.
  - Stay off the ground to avoid shockwaves.

3. The Cursed Warlock (Demonic Sorcerer)

- **Attacks:** Casts elemental spells, summons fire pillars, and warps across the battlefield.
- **Weakness:** Melee attacks disrupt his casting.
- **Strategy:**

- Rush in with **Masha** before he finishes spells.
- Stay mobile to avoid ice spikes and fire zones.
- Use **Kirika's sniper shot** when he retreats to the air.

4. The Demon Lord (Final Boss)

- **Attacks:** Massive sword slashes, summons minions, enters an enraged phase at low health.
- **Weakness:** Weakened briefly after summoning minions.
- **Strategy:**
  - **Use ranged attacks** to deal safe damage in the first phase.
  - Defeat minions quickly to **trigger his stagger state**.
  - **Save energy attacks** for his final enraged form, where he becomes much faster.

5.4 Earning Rewards from Boss Fights

Defeating major bosses in *Gal Guardians: Servants of the Dark* grants valuable **rewards** that enhance gameplay, unlock new abilities, and progress the story.

Types of Rewards

1. **New Abilities**
   - Some bosses drop **unique character upgrades** that unlock **new traversal and combat skills**, such as:
     - **Double Jump:** Allows access to previously unreachable areas.
     - **Elemental Bullets:** Kirika's bullets gain elemental properties (fire, ice, lightning).
     - **Whip Extension:** Increases Masha's melee range.

2. **Health and Energy Upgrades**
   - ○ Bosses often drop **permanent HP or energy boosts**, allowing for longer survival in future battles.
3. **Rare Weapons and Gear**
   - ○ Some fights reward **alternate weapons or enhancements**, such as:
     - ■ **Explosive Crossbow:** A powerful ranged weapon for Kirika.
     - ■ **Demon Slayer Whip:** A stronger version of Masha's standard weapon.
4. **Story Progression & Lore**
   - ○ Defeating bosses reveals **new story segments**, unlocking cutscenes and hidden lore entries.
5. **Unlocking New Areas**
   - ○ Some defeated bosses **remove barriers or curses** blocking off new sections of the **Demon Realm**.

Tips for Maximizing Boss Rewards

- **Use Minimal Healing Items:** Some bosses drop **bonus rewards** for completing the fight without healing.
- **Defeat Bosses Quickly:** Speed-based challenges may grant **extra upgrades** for efficient victories.
- **Explore After Boss Fights:** New pathways often open **immediately after a boss is defeated**.

Chapter 6: Weapons, Items, and Upgrades

6.1 Kirika's Weapons and Enhancements

Kirika specializes in **ranged combat**, using firearms that can be upgraded for increased damage, speed, and special effects. Mastering her arsenal allows for **precise attacks from a safe distance**, making her an essential character in both exploration and combat.

Base Weapon: Spirit Pistols

- **Default dual pistols** with unlimited ammo.
- Fast fire rate but lower damage compared to melee attacks.
- Ideal for **keeping enemies at bay** and attacking airborne foes.

Kirika's Weapon Upgrades

1. **Explosive Rounds**
   - **Effect:** Bullets deal **area-of-effect damage**, making it easier to hit multiple enemies.
   - **Best Use:** Against **clusters of enemies** or breaking destructible barriers.
2. **Piercing Bullets**
   - **Effect:** Shots penetrate through **multiple enemies** and some shields.
   - **Best Use:** Against **armored enemies** and **tight corridors**.
3. **Elemental Ammo**

- Effect: Allows bullets to take on **fire, ice, or lightning** properties.
- **Fire:** Burns enemies over time.
- **Ice:** Slows down enemy movements.
- **Lightning:** Chains between multiple targets.
- **Best Use:** Exploiting **enemy weaknesses** for extra damage.

4. **Rapid-Fire Mode**
   - **Effect:** Increases Kirika's firing speed dramatically, but reduces accuracy.
   - **Best Use: Close-range battles** or against **slow-moving bosses.**

5. **Sniper Mode**
   - **Effect:** Allows Kirika to **charge a powerful shot** that deals massive damage.
   - **Best Use:** Against **stationary targets or bosses with small weak points.**

6. **Homing Bullets**
   - **Effect:** Slightly adjusts bullet trajectory toward the nearest enemy.
   - **Best Use:** Against **fast-moving aerial enemies.**

Enhancements for Kirika

- **Extended Magazine**: Increases **ammo capacity** before reloading.
- **Quick Reload Perk**: Reduces the delay between shots and reload speed.
- **Scope Upgrade**: Adds **zoom functionality** for **precise sniping**.
- **Energy Booster**: Enhances the effectiveness of **special attacks** that use Kirika's energy bar.

6.2 Masha's Weapons and Enhancements

Masha excels in **melee combat**, dealing **high damage at close range**. Her weapons allow for **devastating combos** and special techniques that make her a powerhouse against enemies and bosses.

Base Weapon: Demon Slayer Whip

- Standard melee weapon with **good range and fast attacks**.
- Can perform **combos, aerial strikes, and counterattacks**.
- Effective against **grounded enemies and melee-focused bosses**.

Masha's Weapon Upgrades

1. **Reinforced Whip**
   - **Effect:** Increases base **attack power** and durability.
   - **Best Use:** General combat improvement.
2. **Chain Extension**
   - **Effect:** Increases **whip length**, allowing Masha to hit enemies from **further away**.
   - **Best Use: Mid-range combat** and **hitting multiple enemies at once**.
3. **Elemental Coating**
   - **Effect:** Infuses the whip with **fire, ice, or electricity**.
   - **Fire:** Burns enemies over time.
   - **Ice:** Slows enemy movement.
   - **Electricity:** Stuns enemies momentarily.
   - **Best Use:** To **exploit enemy weaknesses** and add status effects.

4. **Whip Grapple Hook**
   - ○ **Effect:** Allows Masha to **swing across gaps** or **pull enemies toward her**.
   - ○ **Best Use: Traversal** and **crowd control**.
5. **Heavy Strike Mode**
   - ○ **Effect:** Slower attack speed but with **increased knockback and stun power**.
   - ○ **Best Use:** Against **large enemies or shielded foes**.
6. **Whip Spin Attack**
   - ○ **Effect:** Performs a **360-degree attack**, hitting all enemies nearby.
   - ○ **Best Use:** For **clearing swarms of enemies** in tight spaces.

Enhancements for Masha

- **Attack Speed Boost**: Increases **whip attack speed** for faster combos.
- **Armor Break Ability**: Allows her attacks to **break enemy shields** more effectively.
- **Energy Recovery Boost**: Restores more energy when landing **successful melee hits**.
- **Air Combo Mastery**: Enhances Masha's ability to **juggle enemies in mid-air** for extended combos.

6.3 Collectible Items and Their Uses

Throughout *Gal Guardians: Servants of the Dark*, players can find **various collectible items** that aid in combat, exploration, and character progression. Understanding their **effects and best uses** can greatly improve gameplay efficiency.

Healing & Recovery Items

1. **Vitality Elixir**
   - **Effect:** Restores **a portion of HP.**
   - **Best Use: Mid-battle** or before a major encounter to stay alive longer.
2. **Greater Vitality Elixir**
   - **Effect:** Fully restores **Kirika's and Masha's HP.**
   - **Best Use:** Save for **boss fights or tough enemy encounters.**
3. **Energy Crystal**
   - **Effect:** Replenishes **energy used for special abilities.**
   - **Best Use:** Use **before unleashing a powerful attack** to maintain damage output.
4. **Resurrection Token**
   - **Effect:** Revives the fallen sister if one is defeated in battle.
   - **Best Use:** Keep at least one **before boss fights** to prevent game overs.

Combat-Enhancing Items

5. **Demon Fang**
   - **Effect:** Temporarily increases **attack power.**
   - **Best Use:** Use when **entering boss fights** or against powerful mini-bosses.
6. **Guardian Charm**
   - **Effect:** Temporarily **reduces damage taken.**
   - **Best Use:** Ideal for **defensive playstyles** or when facing **strong enemies.**
7. **Swift Feather**
   - **Effect:** Increases movement speed and dodge effectiveness.

- Best Use: Best for **avoiding rapid attacks from fast enemies**.
8. **Blood Pact Scroll**
   - **Effect: Increases critical hit chance** for a limited time.
   - **Best Use:** Use **alongside rapid attacks** to maximize **damage output**.

Exploration & Key Items

9. **Ancient Relics**
   - **Effect:** Unlocks **hidden lore and secrets** within the game.
   - **Best Use:** Gather them to **fully explore the story** and **unlock secret endings**.
10. **Demon Keys**
- **Effect:** Unlocks **sealed doors** leading to hidden areas.
- **Best Use:** Search for **secret locations containing upgrades and rare items**.
11. **Mystic Orbs**
- **Effect:** Activates **special altars** to **reveal hidden paths or unlock new abilities**.
- **Best Use:** Essential for **backtracking and discovering new areas**.
12. **Soul Shards**
- **Effect:** A collectible **currency** used to **purchase upgrades and enhancements**.
- **Best Use:** Save them for **weapon upgrades and skill improvements**.

6.4 Upgrading Your Characters

To survive in the **Demon Realm**, both **Kirika and Masha** must be upgraded to improve their **attack power, defense, and special abilities**. Upgrades can be earned through **combat, exploration, and completing challenges**.

Ways to Upgrade Characters

1. Leveling Up

- Characters **gain experience** from defeating enemies.
- Each level-up provides **small stat boosts** to **health, attack power, and defense**.
- Some **milestone levels unlock new abilities** for each character.

2. Weapon Upgrades

- Weapons can be **enhanced** using **Soul Shards and special materials** found in dungeons.
- Some upgrades **alter weapon properties** (e.g., adding elemental effects or increased damage).

3. Special Ability Unlocks

- Certain **power-ups and relics** unlock new **combat skills**, such as:
    - **Kirika's Multi-Shot:** Allows her to fire multiple bullets in a spread pattern.
    - **Masha's Power Slam:** A heavy downward strike that stuns enemies.

4. Health & Energy Boosts

- Finding **Vital Crystals** increases **maximum HP**, allowing for greater survivability.
- **Energy Crystals** expand the **energy bar**, enabling **more frequent use of special abilities**.

5. Passive Skill Enhancements

- Some **hidden relics** and **shop items** grant **permanent buffs**, such as:
  - Faster **dodge rolls**.
  - Increased **critical hit chance**.
  - Improved **damage resistance**.

6. Mastery Challenges

- Some upgrades are locked behind **combat trials** or **puzzle-based challenges**.
- Completing them **rewards special abilities or unique gear** that cannot be obtained elsewhere.

Chapter 7: Multiplayer and Co-op Gameplay

7.1 Local and Online Co-op Mode

Gal Guardians: Servants of the Dark features a **cooperative multiplayer mode** that allows two players to control **Kirika and Masha simultaneously**. This mode enhances gameplay by introducing **team-based strategies, shared abilities, and unique co-op interactions**.

Local Co-op

- Players can team up using **split controllers or two separate controllers** on the same device.
- **Drop-in/drop-out functionality** lets a second player join or leave at any time.
- Allows for **better coordination and faster progression** compared to solo play.

Online Co-op

- Players can connect via **online matchmaking** or invite friends for **private co-op sessions**.
- Communication is key—use **voice chat or quick commands** to coordinate attacks.
- Some **latency issues may affect timing-based mechanics**, so stable internet is recommended.

7.2 Character Synergy and Teamwork

In multiplayer mode, **Kirika and Masha must work together**, utilizing their strengths to overcome difficult challenges.

Kirika's Role (Ranged Support & Crowd Control)

- Provides **long-range damage** and keeps enemies at a distance.
- Can **weaken enemies** before Masha moves in for close combat.
- **Best suited for defensive playstyles**, avoiding direct hits while providing cover fire.

Masha's Role (Melee Combat & Tanking)

- Specializes in **high-damage melee attacks** that break enemy defenses.
- Can **draw enemy aggro**, allowing Kirika to attack safely from afar.
- **Best for aggressive players** who like close combat.

Synergy Moves & Co-op Mechanics

- **Dual Assault Combo**: When both players attack the same enemy simultaneously, they deal **bonus damage**.
- **Quick Swap Strategy**: If one player is low on health, they can **let their partner take the lead** while recovering.
- **Trap Handling**: Masha can **trigger levers and break obstacles**, while Kirika provides **cover fire** against lurking enemies.

7.3 Best Strategies for Two-Player Mode

1. Balanced Offense & Defense

- Let **Masha engage enemies upfront**, while **Kirika attacks from a safe distance**.
- If an enemy focuses on **Kirika**, have **Masha intercept and take control** of the fight.

2. Synchronizing Special Abilities

- If one player activates a **special attack**, the other should **immediately follow up** to chain combos.
- Use **Kirika's elemental bullets** to weaken enemies before **Masha's finishing strikes**.

3. Reviving & Survival Tactics

- If one player falls, the remaining player must **find a safe moment** to revive them.
- Always **keep a Resurrection Token** available in case of emergencies.

4. Splitting Up for Exploration

- Some levels have **split-path puzzles** that require both players to activate switches or uncover hidden paths.
- Communicate clearly to **ensure both players know their objectives**.

7.4 Challenges and Rewards in Co-op Play

Playing in **co-op mode** introduces **special challenges and exclusive rewards** that **aren't available in solo mode.**

Co-op Exclusive Challenges

- **Synchronized Platforming**: Some areas require **both players to activate platforms together**.
- **Timed Combat Trials**: Enemies may **spawn in waves**, forcing both players to **clear them within a time limit**.
- **Team-Based Puzzles**: Some dungeons require **dual lever activations** or **coordinated movements** to progress.

Co-op Rewards

- **Bonus Experience**: Playing in co-op grants **slightly more XP** for faster character upgrades.
- **Special Weapons**: Some unique **co-op-only weapons and gear** are available through multiplayer challenges.
- **Hidden Lore & Cutscenes**: Some **dialogue and story interactions change** depending on **team dynamics**.

Hard Mode & Competitive Play

- After completing the main story, co-op players can unlock **"Hard Mode"**, where enemies have **enhanced abilities**.
- A **competitive scoring system** can be enabled, tracking each player's **kills, damage output, and combo chains**.

Chapter 8: Secrets, Easter Eggs, and Unlockables

8.1 Hidden Items and Secret Areas

Throughout *Gal Guardians: Servants of the Dark*, players can discover **hidden items and secret areas** that provide **valuable rewards, lore expansions, and gameplay enhancements**. These secrets often require **keen exploration, puzzle-solving, and backtracking** to access.

How to Find Secret Areas

- **Breakable Walls:** Some walls can be **destroyed using Masha's melee attacks** or **Kirika's explosive bullets**.
- **Hidden Passages:** Certain areas have **illusory walls or invisible platforms** that require careful exploration.
- **Environmental Clues:** Some hidden areas are marked by **subtle cracks, unusual symbols, or out-of-place objects**.
- **Backtracking with New Abilities:** Some paths can only be accessed after **unlocking certain abilities** later in the game.

Notable Hidden Items & Their Locations

1. **Demon Crest Relics**
   - Unlocks **lore entries** and **special abilities** when collected.
   - Found in **hard-to-reach areas requiring platforming skills**.
2. **Mystic Orbs**

- Used to **unlock new abilities** for Kirika and Masha.
- Often hidden behind **puzzle-locked doors**.

3. **Rare Soul Shards**
   - Grants a large amount of **upgrade currency** for weapons and skills.
   - Usually found **behind mini-bosses or within secret rooms**.

4. **Legendary Weapons**
   - Some of the **strongest weapons in the game** are hidden in **optional dungeons**.
   - Requires **solving difficult platforming or combat challenges** to obtain.

5. **Alternate Endings & Secret Bosses**
   - Some secret areas **lead to hidden bosses**, which may **unlock new endings** if defeated.
   - Requires **completing special objectives**, such as collecting **all Demon Crest Relics**.

8.2 Unlockable Costumes and Skins

Players can unlock **alternative costumes and skins** for **Kirika and Masha** by **completing specific objectives, finding collectibles, or meeting secret requirements**.

How to Unlock Costumes

- **Completing the Main Story:** Some costumes unlock automatically after finishing the game.
- **Finding Secret Collectibles:** Certain costumes require **collecting rare items** hidden throughout the game.
- **Beating Special Challenges:** Time trials, boss rush modes, or hard difficulty runs unlock exclusive outfits.

Unlockable Costumes & How to Get Them

1. **Classic School Uniforms**
   - **How to Unlock:** Available by default.
2. **Battle-Damaged Outfits**
   - **How to Unlock:** Complete the game on **Normal Mode**.
3. **Demon Hunter Armor**
   - **How to Unlock:** Defeat all **secret bosses** in the game.
   - **Effect:** Increases **damage resistance** slightly.
4. **Dark Sorceress Kirika & Shadow Knight Masha**
   - **How to Unlock:** Complete the game on **Hard Mode** without using any continues.
   - **Effect:** Grants **aesthetic changes with glowing effects**.
5. **Retro Pixel Skins**
   - **How to Unlock:** Collect **all Mystic Orbs** hidden throughout the game.
   - **Effect:** Changes the character sprites to **16-bit retro designs**.
6. **Holiday & Seasonal Skins**
   - **How to Unlock:** Can be found in **special seasonal events or DLC content**.

8.3 Special Challenges and Extra Modes

Beyond the main story, *Gal Guardians: Servants of the Dark* offers **special challenges and extra gameplay modes** that test players' skills and reward them with unique items and achievements. These modes introduce **harder enemy encounters, time-based trials, and remixed versions of levels**.

Special Challenges

1. **Boss Rush Mode**
   - Unlocks after **completing the main game**.
   - Players must **fight all major bosses back-to-back** without checkpoints.
   - Rewards: **Exclusive weapon skins and high-score rankings**.
2. **Speedrun Mode**
   - Timer-based mode where players **race against the clock** to finish the game as quickly as possible.
   - Includes **leaderboards for best completion times**.
   - Rewards: **Speedrunner title and unique effects for characters**.
3. **Survival Gauntlet**
   - A wave-based challenge where players must **defeat endless waves of enemies**.
   - Enemies grow **stronger over time**, making each round tougher.
   - Rewards: **Rare upgrade materials and special titles**.
4. **No-Hit Challenge**
   - Requires players to **complete levels or boss fights without taking any damage**.
   - Extremely difficult but **grants rare costumes and weapons**.

Extra Modes

1. **Hardcore Mode (One-Life Permadeath)**
   - Players have **only one life**—if they die, the run ends.
   - Enemies deal **double damage**, and healing items are **scarce**.

- Rewards: **"Demon Slayer" title and the strongest weapon in the game.**
2. **Nightmare Mode (Enemy Remixes & Level Changes)**
   - Enemies have **new attack patterns,** and **platforming sections are more challenging.**
   - Some bosses **gain extra phases,** making fights significantly harder.
   - Rewards: **Secret ending and exclusive armor set.**
3. **Alternate Story Mode**
   - A special version of the story where **events play out differently** based on hidden choices.
   - Features **new dialogue, boss encounters, and additional cutscenes.**
   - Rewards: **A different ending and lore expansion.**

8.4 Developer Easter Eggs and References

The developers of *Gal Guardians: Servants of the Dark* have hidden **various Easter eggs, inside jokes, and references** to other games, anime, and pop culture.

Hidden Developer Messages & Secrets

1. **Developer Room**
   - Hidden in a **secret section of the map,** players can find a room containing **portraits and notes from the developers.**
   - Includes **funny commentary, behind-the-scenes trivia, and secret lore clues.**
2. **Classic Metroidvania References**

- Certain **level designs, enemy animations, and power-ups** pay homage to **classic games like Castlevania and Metroid**.
- A particular **enemy boss has an attack pattern resembling a famous Castlevania boss**.

3. **Anime & Pop Culture Callbacks**
   - Some character costumes and dialogue reference **popular anime and manga series**.
   - Kirika's **victory pose mimics a famous magical girl transformation**.

4. **Hidden Character Cameos**
   - Some NPCs resemble **characters from previous games by the developers**.
   - Players who have played past titles may recognize **familiar faces in the background**.

5. **Fourth Wall Breaks & Funny Interactions**
   - Certain interactions between Kirika and Masha **break the fourth wall**, acknowledging they are in a game.
   - Some item descriptions **contain self-aware humor**, hinting at the development process.

Chapter 9: Tips, Tricks, and Advanced Strategies

9.1 Best Tactics for Speedrunning

Speedrunning *Gal Guardians: Servants of the Dark* requires **precise movement, enemy manipulation, and efficient route planning**. Here are some key strategies to help you complete the game in record time.

Optimizing Movement

- **Dash Cancelling**: Use **Kirika's dodge and Masha's dash ability** to move faster than normal running speed.
- **Jump Momentum**: Certain jumps **carry more speed** if executed at the right timing—use this to skip sections.
- **Animation Skipping**: Some attacks and abilities can **cancel slow animations**, saving time.

Combat Efficiency

- **Avoid Unnecessary Fights**: Only defeat **mandatory enemies and mini-bosses**—ignore others to save time.
- **Quick Kill Bosses**: Memorize **boss patterns** to maximize **damage output and minimize fight duration**.
- **Preemptive Attack Strategies**: Enter boss fights **with full SP meter** to unleash **high-damage skills instantly**.

Route Optimization

- **Know Key Item Locations**: Plan ahead to collect only **essential upgrades** while skipping unnecessary detours.
- **Use Sequence Breaks**: Some movement exploits allow you to **bypass obstacles earlier than intended**.
- **Use Fast Travel Smartly**: Activate **key checkpoints** to backtrack efficiently without wasting time.

Recommended Speedrun Category Goals

- **Any% Run**: Finish the game as fast as possible, even with glitches.
- **100% Run**: Collect **all upgrades and secrets** while maintaining an optimal route.

9.2 How to Maximize Your Score and Rewards

Scoring high in *Gal Guardians* depends on **combat efficiency, exploration, and completing challenges**.

Increasing Combat Score

- **Maintain Combos**: Chaining attacks without getting hit **increases your score multiplier**.
- **Perfect Dodges**: Dodging **at the last second** grants bonus points.
- **Defeating Enemies Quickly**: Fast kills result in **higher score rankings per encounter**.

Maximizing Rewards

- **Explore Every Area**: Some of the best **weapons and upgrades** are in hidden locations.
- **Complete Side Quests**: NPCs may offer **rare items** for helping them.
- **Replay Boss Battles**: Some bosses give **extra loot** if defeated under specific conditions (e.g., no damage taken).

Farming Techniques

- **Enemy Respawn Spots**: Some areas have **fast enemy respawns**, making them good for XP and loot grinding.
- **Special Challenge Rooms**: Certain secret rooms have **bonus fights** that drop valuable items.
- **Timed Challenges**: Some levels **reward players for speed-clearing sections**.

9.3 Avoiding Common Mistakes

Even experienced players can make **critical errors** that slow progression, increase difficulty, or result in unnecessary deaths. Avoid these common pitfalls to improve your gameplay experience.

Combat Mistakes

- **Ignoring Character Strengths**: Kirika excels at **ranged combat**, while Masha is a **melee powerhouse**. Failing to switch between them **at the right moments** can make fights harder.
- **Overusing SP Attacks**: Special abilities are **powerful but limited**—save them for **tougher enemies and bosses** rather than wasting them on weak mobs.

- **Not Learning Enemy Patterns**: Every enemy has a **set attack pattern**. Rushing in without **studying their behavior** will result in **avoidable damage**.
- **Forgetting to Dodge and Block**: Dodging and blocking reduce incoming damage. Failing to use these mechanics will drain your health quickly.

Exploration Mistakes

- **Skipping Important Upgrades**: Certain weapons and abilities **make later stages significantly easier**. Always search for upgrades before progressing too far.
- **Not Using the Map Effectively**: The in-game map marks **hidden rooms, shortcuts, and backtracking opportunities**. Players who don't check their map **may miss key areas**.
- **Rushing Through Levels**: The game encourages **thorough exploration**. Skipping side paths **can mean missing powerful items** and **bonus fights**.
- **Underestimating Environmental Hazards**: Some areas contain **traps, crumbling platforms, or poison zones—** not paying attention can result in **avoidable deaths**.

Progression Mistakes

- **Not Saving Regularly**: Save points are **limited**. Failing to save before a **tough boss fight** could force you to restart a long section.
- **Wasting Healing Items Too Early**: Learn **enemy attack patterns** so you **take minimal damage**, reducing the need to use health-restoring items.
- **Not Upgrading Weapons & Abilities**: Some players stick with **starting weapons** for too long—upgrade them as soon as possible to **keep up with stronger enemies**.

Co-op Mode Mistakes

- **Lack of Coordination**: In multiplayer, failing to **communicate with your partner** leads to **inefficient attacks and wasted resources**.
- **Ignoring Character Synergy**: One player should focus on **damage dealing**, while the other provides **support and strategic positioning**.

9.4 Expert Strategies for Hardcore Players

For those attempting **Hard Mode, Nightmare Mode, or One-Life Permadeath**, mastering these **expert-level strategies** will ensure success.

Advanced Combat Tactics

- **Frame-Perfect Dodging**: Perfectly timed dodges grant **temporary invincibility**—use this against **high-damage boss attacks**.
- **Parry & Counterattack**: Some enemy attacks can be **parried**, creating an opening for a **devastating counterattack**.
- **Hitbox Exploitation**: Certain attacks leave **small safe zones**—position yourself carefully to avoid damage while still landing hits.
- **SP Meter Optimization**: Instead of **using SP randomly**, save it for **critical moments in boss fights or enemy swarms**.

Surviving One-Life Permadeath Mode

- **Prioritize Defense Over Offense**: Playing aggressively is risky—focus on **survival and avoiding damage first**.
- **Master Every Boss Fight**: Memorizing **each boss's attack patterns** allows you to anticipate moves **before they happen**.
- **Plan Your Upgrade Path Carefully**: Certain weapons and abilities **scale better** in tougher modes—choose upgrades that increase **survivability** over raw damage.
- **Use Checkpoints Wisely**: Plan **which areas to save progress in** to avoid repeating difficult sections.

Perfect Boss Fights

- **Memorize Attack Patterns**: Every boss follows a **predictable sequence**—knowing what comes next **prevents unnecessary damage**.
- **Exploit Weaknesses**: Some bosses are **weak to specific attacks or abilities**—adjust your strategy accordingly.
- **Time Your Special Attacks**: Use **SP attacks during a boss's vulnerability window** to maximize damage.

Sequence Breaking & Speedrun Tricks

- **Skipping Non-Essential Fights**: If a battle isn't **required for progression**, **avoid it entirely**.
- **Exploiting Movement Mechanics**: Some platforming techniques allow **early access to key areas**, bypassing challenges.
- **Fast Boss Kills**: Learn **quick kill strats** for each major boss to **cut down fight duration**.

Chapter 10: Conclusion and Final Thoughts

10.1 Summary of Key Takeaways

Throughout this guide, we've covered everything from **basic mechanics to advanced strategies**, helping players of all skill levels master *Gal Guardians: Servants of the Dark*. Below is a **recap of the most important aspects** to keep in mind:

Core Gameplay & Mechanics

- **Kirika and Masha's unique playstyles**: Kirika specializes in **ranged attacks**, while Masha excels in **melee combat**.
- **Switching characters effectively** is key to overcoming enemies and obstacles.
- **Managing SP and special attacks wisely** can make a big difference in tough battles.
- **Utilizing fast travel and backtracking** helps uncover secret paths and hidden upgrades.

Combat & Boss Battles

- **Understanding enemy attack patterns** allows for better dodging and counterattacks.
- **Perfectly timed dodges and blocks** can make battles much easier, especially in **harder difficulties**.
- **Boss fights require strategic planning**—saving SP for their toughest phases is crucial.
- **Upgrading weapons and abilities** early helps with progression.

Exploration & Secrets

- **Pay attention to environmental clues**—some walls and platforms hide secrets.
- **Collecting hidden items and completing side quests** unlocks powerful upgrades.
- **Alternative routes and sequence breaks** can make certain sections faster or easier.

Multiplayer & Co-op Mode

- **Team synergy is key**—coordinate attacks and defensive maneuvers with your partner.
- **Some areas and challenges are easier in co-op**, while others require **careful teamwork**.
- **Co-op-exclusive rewards** make playing with a friend worth trying.

Advanced Play & Challenges

- **Speedrunning requires optimized movement and boss strategies**.
- **Hardcore mode demands patience, precision, and deep knowledge of enemy patterns**.
- **Unlockable content and Easter eggs add additional replay value**.

10.2 Post-Game Content and Replayability

Once you've completed the main story, *Gal Guardians: Servants of the Dark* offers **a variety of post-game content** to keep you engaged.

Unlockable Modes & Challenges

- **Boss Rush Mode**: Face all major bosses in a **gauntlet-style battle** with no checkpoints.
- **Survival Challenge**: Endless waves of enemies test your endurance and skill.
- **Hardcore & Nightmare Modes**: More difficult settings with **remixed enemy behavior and limited resources.**

New Game Plus (NG+)

- **Carry over weapons, upgrades, and abilities** from your first playthrough.
- **Enemies and bosses become stronger**, but **new rewards and hidden content** become available.
- **Unlock alternative endings** based on choices made in NG+.

Hidden Collectibles & Alternate Paths

- **Some areas and bosses are only accessible after the first playthrough.**
- **Finding all secrets unlocks powerful weapons, costumes, and lore expansions.**

Replayability & Different Playstyles

- **Try a "no-hit" or speedrun challenge** for an extra layer of difficulty.
- **Experiment with different upgrade paths** to create unique playthrough experiences.
- **Co-op mode offers a fresh perspective**, especially with a skilled partner.

10.3 Community and Online Resources

For players looking to **dive deeper into the game**, connect with other fans, or find **additional tips and strategies**, the *Gal Guardians: Servants of the Dark* community offers plenty of **resources and discussions**.

Official and Fan Communities

- **Official Forums & Websites**: Check the game's **official website and developer forums** for patch notes, announcements, and discussions.
- **Reddit & Discord Servers**: Join **fan-made communities** to share experiences, strategies, and discoveries.
- **Social Media Groups**: Follow game-related **Facebook groups, Twitter hashtags, and YouTube channels** for updates and discussions.

Gameplay Guides & Wiki Pages

- **Fan Wikis**: Websites like **Fandom Wikis** provide detailed breakdowns of **weapons, enemies, hidden items, and lore**.
- **Speedrun Leaderboards**: Platforms like **Speedrun.com** track the fastest completion times, including **speedrun strategies and skips**.
- **YouTube Walkthroughs & Twitch Streams**: Watch **pro players and streamers** to learn advanced techniques and boss strategies.

Modding and Custom Content

- Some fans create **custom skins, challenges, and difficulty mods** for the game.
- Check community hubs like **Steam Workshop (if available)** for **fan-made content**.

Reporting Bugs & Providing Feedback

- Players can report issues and suggest improvements via **official bug-tracking forums** or developer email support.
- Some developers consider **fan feedback for balancing patches** and future updates.

10.4 Future Updates and Potential DLC

While *Gal Guardians: Servants of the Dark* is already a **content-rich experience**, the potential for **future updates and DLC expansions** could bring even more excitement.

Possible Future Updates

- **Bug Fixes & Balance Adjustments**: Developers often release **patches to fine-tune gameplay mechanics** based on community feedback.
- **New Game Modes**: Possible additions like **Time Attack Mode, Endless Survival, or Randomizer Mode** could enhance replayability.
- **Additional Difficulty Levels**: Introducing **Ultra Nightmare or Custom Difficulty settings** could challenge veteran players.

Potential DLC Expansions

If the developers release **DLC (Downloadable Content)**, it could include:

- **New Playable Characters**: Expanding the roster with **additional heroes with unique abilities**.
- **Extra Story Content**: New **chapters or side quests** that expand the lore of the game.
- **Bonus Weapons & Upgrades**: Exclusive weapons, skills, or transformation abilities.
- **Challenge Dungeons**: New high-level areas with **tougher enemies and powerful rewards**.
- **Co-op Enhancements**: Additional multiplayer features, such as **PvP battles or new co-op challenges**.

How to Stay Updated

- Follow the **official game website, Twitter, and Discord** for announcements.
- Check **developer interviews and press releases** for hints about upcoming content.
- Watch **gaming news sites and YouTube gaming channels** for early information on potential expansions.

www.ingramcontent.com/pod-product-compliance
Lightning Source LLC
LaVergne TN
LVHW051609050326
832903LV00033B/4414